Praise for *Time for Wonder*

"Beautiful and timely... *Time for Wonder* is a breath of fresh air. Its timeless message of slowing down and being present is presented in a multidimensional format that is uplifting and nurturing. This work is a great companion for living a beautiful, flowing life of abundance and gratitude."

—E.H. Rick Jarow, Ph.D.
Associate Professor of Religious Studies, Vassar College
Author of *The Alchemy of Abundance* and *Creating the Work You Love*

"This little book is a treasure chest of wonder! Listening to Cathy's song while drinking in the colors, shapes and textures of nature on each page feels like a soul bath, a respite, an immediate deep breath of release and opening. While this world is full of wonder, we take too little time to honor it. This book honors it abundantly."

—Lynn Koerbel, MPH
Assistant Director, MBSR Teacher Education & Curricula Development
Mindfulness Center, Brown University, School of Professional Studies

"In *Time for Wonder*, Cathy Sacco offers a book that will never grow old; it is a companion on a journey of mindful moments filled with wonder. The gentleness of the invitation offered to the reader triggered my curiosity. I was drawn to its simplicity; the limited words and the pictures helped to slow me down and go inside. The additional practices at the end inspired me to go off in my own direction and discovery. This is a beautiful book. There are many layers, enjoy them all."

—Paul Davis, author of *A Way of Life, Zen Monastics at Work and Play*,
Order of Interbeing member and leader of Being Peace Sangha of Cincinnati

"These little verses and images might seem simple, but you'd be mistaken. The phrases, guidance and striking photography are the end result of years of practice, attentiveness, and, of course, wonder. *Time for Wonder* is what all great books should be, a reminder of a different way of living... in our bodies, in nature, in the world."

—Francis Salzano, Ph.D.
Author of *Zen Of The Wild, A Philosophy for Nature*

"What a life-changing way to start your day or recharge when you are feeling overwhelmed. *Time for Wonder* is an unexpected, very simple way to meditate. It can be difficult to shut down the stream of thoughts in my head and as I turned each page, gazing at the calm, beautiful pictures, I connected more with my breath and felt the stress in my body release. The photographs and words are not just beautiful, they are highly symbolic, reaching into your unconscious soul in a powerful way. I will be recommending this to clients and friends."

—Katie Beecher
Medical & Spiritual Intuitive and Licensed Counselor
Author of *Heal from Within: A Guidebook to Intuitive Wellness*

"Discovering *Time for Wonder* felt like taking a slow, deep breath after a frantic day. Paging through, I felt myself relax into the stunning images paired with lines lifted from the song the book is named for. (Don't skip downloading the song, which is included with the book!) 'Ask yourself what makes your own heart sing,' author Cathy Sacco urges, pulling me away from the noise of modern life and back to what truly matters—to that deeper kind of wonder that lies within us. I especially love the Simple Practices that are geared to reconnecting with wonder moment by moment. As a writer, visual artist and mindfulness practitioner, I know this book will live in my backpack, along with my sketch journal."

—Elaine Olund, author of *The Invisible Suitcase* (poems), Finishing Line Press

"This song, both the lyrics and melody, calms my soul and mind. I'd like to have it as my 'wake up' every morning. Our lives are bombarded with so much noise, chaos and technology every day. *Time for Wonder* helps us return to our true, beautiful center. I especially want to share this song and book with my grandchildren."

—M.K. Hurley, Visual Artist and Teacher

"Cathy Sacco's book *Time for Wonder* takes you on a journey connecting body, mind and soul to the natural beauty that surrounds us all. The book is more than meditation, it is a work of art meant to be experienced. Coupled with the beautifully penned lyrics of the same name, *Time for Wonder* is just that, a time to set aside all of the "doings" of life and replace them with the simple act of "being," allowing us to again sit in wonder of the beauty all around us. I especially appreciate the wonderful suggestions in the back of the book about how to incorporate wonder into our everyday lives. I highly recommend this timely work."

—Mark Miller
Founder/Owner Pendleton Consulting

"I hold this book of wonder, as I do mala beads. Each page connects me to awe, enhances my practice of learning to pay attention to the world. Grateful to have such a tool to enhance my inner life."

—Mary Pierce Brosmer
Founder, Women Writing for (a) Change

"This poem and book are rich and stunningly beautiful! The message is timeless and much needed in our culture."

—Heidi Bright, Coach, Editor, and Author of *Thriver Soup,*
A Feast for Living Consciously During the Cancer Journey

Time for Wonder

Time for Wonder

CATHY SACCO

This book is dedicated to John, Emma and Allie, who have supported me unconditionally in my quest for creative expression, truth and beauty, and to my parents who gave me the gift of love and unstructured time to think, to be, and to create.

"Wisdom begins in wonder."
—Socrates

It was a sparkling fall day as I was leaving a meditation retreat and driving the back roads toward western Massachusetts. I became mesmerized by the stunning beauty of the turning trees in afternoon light and wanted to express this wordless connection. I paused and listened to what I felt, and then began to hum and make up a tune. During that two-hour ride a song poured out. Over the next months I finished the music and lyrics, and made the recording. The content and process seemed to emerge suddenly, yet I knew the seeds had been planted long ago below the surface, active yet unseen.

Listen to "Time for Wonder"
Written and Recorded by the Author

www.cathysacco.com/music/

INTRODUCTION

This book is an invitation to slow down and see more. It is only by first slowing down our busy-ness and constant doing that we are able to begin hearing our own heartbeat, seeing the beauty of a snowflake falling, the subtle changes of a sunrise, or sensing the natural rhythms in the natural world. In our rapid culture, it is very easy to succumb to our constantly thinking and judging minds.

I was fortunate to experience plenty of down-time in my childhood. This spaciousness helped me connect not only to a creative life, but to a sense of wonder. Over time it beckoned me to discover the unknown, and to feel gratitude and reverence, especially for small things. Now I feel its presence often when I am alone in stillness, during walks in nature, while humming tunes of unknown origin, and during sudden moments of insight. I hold this sense of wonder, reflecting on it as an important seed of intuition for what makes me feel connected, alive and purposeful.

"Live the actual moment. Only this moment is life."

—Thich Nhat Hanh

REFLECT ON THE VERSES

Each verse is a reminder of what is simple yet profound in everyday life that we may easily overlook in our busy lives. Listen to the song, preferably in nature but anywhere will do. Allow the music and words to wash over you.

Enjoy it as a whole or choose a phrase that speaks to you. Pin it up, write it down, journal and create art about it. Let its meaning inspire and inform your day or week. You might wish to teach the words to your children and grandchildren, your students or friends, and sing it with them. Ask them to reflect, express, and discuss how it makes them feel.

BEHOLDING IMAGES: A VISUAL MEDITATION PRACTICE

Find a few images in the book that attract you, and slowly focus on them one at a time. Soften your gaze and behold each image for at least a minute or more. Through this intentional practice of becoming more familiar with something, or someone, we can grow in connection, empathy and compassion.

Use the images as focal points. Relax the mind by not thinking or analyzing too much. Focus on the whole image, then the parts: the lines, shapes, textures, patterns and colors, and then the whole again to feel its essence. Let the images imprint and stay with you. You might reflect, journal or draw what you discover and feel. Then collect your own images, ideas and metaphors to savor for a life filled with moments of wonder!

And every once in a while, ask yourself what makes your own heart sing, and do not forget it.

"It is the looking at things for a long time that ripens you and gives you a deeper understanding."

—Vincent van Gogh

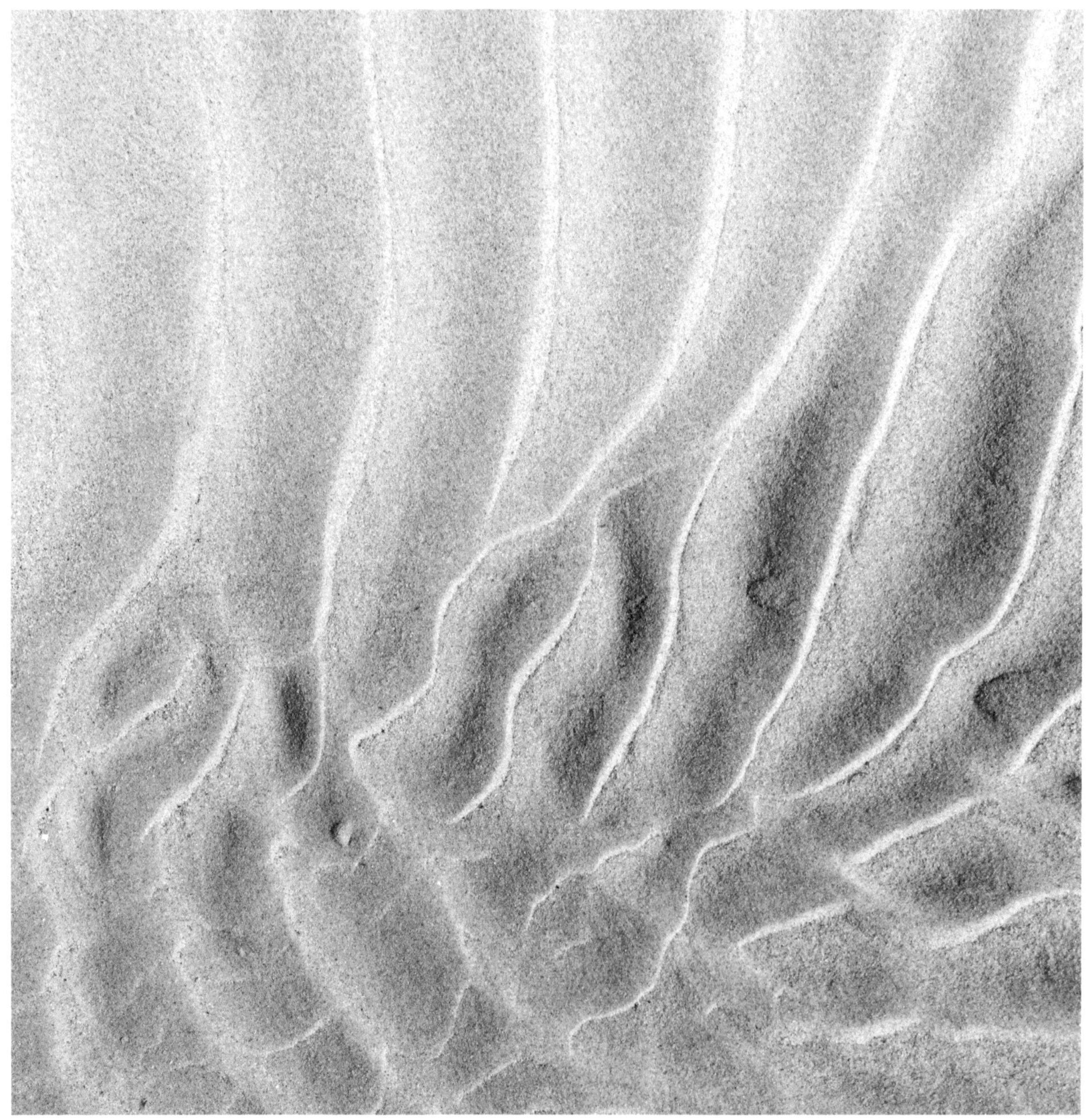

TIME FOR WONDER

Take Time for Wonder
Slow Yourself Down
Touch the Blue Sky
The Leaves on the Ground

Take Time for Wonder
You'll Know the Way
It's Close to Your Heart
And It's in Every Day

Moment by Moment
You'll See the Signs
Birds on the Branch
And Bees in the Hive

Be Very Still
And Hear Every Tree
Feel the Wind Blow
It Will Help You Be Free

Watching a Flower
Unfolding with Grace
See So Much More
When You Slow Down the Pace

Water the Garden
And Each Different Seed
Everyone Blooms
When They Have What They Need

Notice the Sunlight
Shining So Bright
Feet on the Earth
And Your Mind Like the Sky

Step Back and Pause
Focus Inside
Take a Deep Breath
And Your Heart Opens Wide

You Might Think it Will Last...
But We Only have this Moment to Treasure

Take Time for Wonder
Slow Yourself Down
Planting the Seeds
Of Love All Around

Take Time for Wonder
You'll Know the Way
It's Close to Your Heart
And It's in Every Day

TAKE TIME FOR WONDER

Slow Yourself Down

TOUCH THE BLUE SKY

The Leaves on the Ground

TAKE TIME FOR WONDER

YOU'LL KNOW THE WAY

It's Close to Your Heart

And It's in Every Day

Moment by Moment

You'll See the Signs

Birds on the Branch

And Bees in the Hive

Be Very Still

And Hear Every Tree

Feel the Wind Blow

It Will Help You Be Free

Watching a Flower

Unfolding with Grace

See So Much More

When You Slow Down the Pace

WATER THE GARDEN AND EACH DIFFERENT SEED

Everyone Blooms

WHEN THEY HAVE WHAT THEY NEED

Notice the Sunlight

Shining So Bright

Feet on the Earth

And Your Mind Like the Sky

Step Back and Pause

FOCUS INSIDE

Take a Deep Breath

And Your Heart Opens Wide

You Might Think It Will Last...

BUT WE ONLY HAVE THIS MOMENT
TO TREASURE

Take Time for Wonder

Slow Yourself Down

Planting the Seeds of Love All Around

Take Time for Wonder

You'll Know the Way

It's Close to Your Heart

AND IT'S IN EVERY DAY

PERCEPTION AND CONNECTION

The kind of wonder most familiar in our Western culture is common in many classrooms, and involves asking questions to find out more about something. There is a second, deeper kind of wonder that is more like a state of being. It rests below our thinking mind and cannot be grasped, willed or planned. It is a sacred place to be and an antecedent to wisdom and consciousness.

When we tune into our senses and intuition, we rest our conscious mind and create space to receive something more sublime, and perhaps more important. I have found that this 'something' fuels our reverence for the sacred, our innate curiosity for the unknown, and for connection.

Every one of us has a unique rhythm, a pattern, a deeper pulse or song that's imprinted. It might get pushed to the background, yet it lives inside us like a seed of potential waiting for the right conditions to unfold and thrive.

When we slow down we start to become aware of the daily chatter in our mind and can then let it settle. Through intention and awareness, what we previously passed by in a rush, or took for granted, may start to fill out with more detail. Our perception and awareness becomes keener, and more expansive. We are able to develop a beginner's mind where preconceptions drop away. We are more available to glimpse the extraordinary within the very ordinary.

It's as if the world starts to present itself to us with sheer delight. Yet it has always been there, waiting for us to be ready.

PLAY AND CURIOSITY

Being in a state of wonder involves a playful attitude that is not concerned with knowing or being certain. Young people especially need time and space to explore and make choices in order to remain curious and learn to trust their own direct experiences and feelings. As an artist, I have valued this process of making choices and decisions which has helped cultivate my intuition. As adults, we can learn from this and shift our lens toward curiosity in any moment.

Maintaining our playful curiosity helps us to pause and appreciate what we encounter in the moment. This attitude may also protect us from unnecessary chronic stress emanating from ruminating thoughts and habitual patterns of reactivity which can contribute to physical illness over time, and rob us of ease and joy.

Rooted in ancient Eastern and Buddhist philosophies, mindfulness meditation is the intentional practice of paying attention on purpose in the present moment with an attitude of gentleness and curiosity, rather than internal or external judgement. Curiosity is essential for imagination and creativity. It helps our minds pause from immediate judgment, analysis, aversion or attachment to what we want or expect. This practice of aligning with curiosity sidesteps old patterns and cultivates a type of courage and mental clarity to be in the world with more empathy, creative capacity, and mindful engagement.

"Value judgments are destructive to our proper business which is one of curiosity and awareness."

—John Cage

REDISCOVER YOUR INNER COMPASS

Authentic learning requires space and permission to try things, to make mistakes and to be in the unknown. We can learn from watching children as they do this naturally and unselfconsciously. Young children are generally not as encumbered by past failures, mistakes, or the judgments of others and follow a direct path to what their hearts are called to. They persist for the joy of the process. If something doesn't work, they try again. Or try differently. This playful energy is all-absorbing and essential to authentic discovery and learning. Cultivating it can help us be more comfortable with the unknown.

The spaciousness for discovery, however, is removed far too quickly from our lives in favor of certainty and knowing. Most of us have little unstructured time in a culture that honors speed, accomplishment, and perfection. This paradigm begins as early as grade school and can squash natural curiosity, creativity, and desire. From an early age we are told what to do and when to do it. While rooted in the good intentions of adults, this may contribute to lost confidence in our own perceptions, thoughts and feelings.

Many of us acquire a compass early on that is externally driven. This may include thoughts like "Must plan, must do well, must do more, must have the right answers." These internal thoughts can evolve into a fear of being judged, left behind, or feeling that we are not enough as we are. If we are taught only to follow the instructions of others rather than to lead ourselves, it becomes a practice to remember how to be comfortable in trying out new things and making mistakes rather than quickly moving toward a goal.

While analyzing, categorizing, comparing, and evaluating are valued higher level cognitive skills useful in learning and making good decisions, these very processes on their own may shrink the spaciousness needed for imagination. They can create a kind of duality which separates us from each other, from nature, and from connection with our whole self. When we slow down and begin to notice things and people on purpose with full awareness, we can experience their essence without labeling or judging. This observational practice interrupts our habitual patterns and builds transformative connections in the brain that can actually reduce prejudice and increase perspective and empathy—two important elements of emotional intelligence.

Authentic learning requires time and space to try and retry new things, to ponder and reflect, and to let go of judgment about the outcome. Here we can be very present to our own discoveries and then let them rest and transform. While we often discount this process as nothing much, there is great value in taking time with early steps of exploration. These steps are the basis for rich new soil of the imagination, joy of learning and a fulfilling life. They contain certain elements of intuition and knowing. As author Joanna Macy said, "There's a song that wants to sing itself through us, and we've just got to be available."

By allowing ourselves to take time with these experiences and be changed by them, we open the door to wonder.

SIMPLE PRACTICES

Try some of these beginning exercises on your own. You can mix them up and do most of them sitting or standing or even lying down, indoors or outdoors. If you don't have access to nature, you might even adopt a house plant or a view outside a window, but this is not necessary. Have patience with yourself as you slowly try the practices, and come back to them often. Your sense of awareness will continue to develop over time.

- Slow down: Notice your body, your breath, your mind.

- Feel the weight of your body on the earth, chair, or wherever you are. Feel the sensation of your feet on the ground.

- Sense the temperature, texture, and shifting movement of the air and how it feels on your skin moment to moment.

- Notice any scents in the environment, like the fragrance of a flower or the earthiness of the leaves and soil. Is there something more?

- Begin to notice where the breath comes in and out through the nose. Sense its temperature and pace. Notice how your belly naturally rises and falls with each breath cycle.

- Listen for sounds or layers of sound near and far, like birdsong, the crunch of stones or leaves underfoot, the wind through the trees, the sound of an animal scurrying, voices, or even an airplane. See if you can place attention on individual sounds as you become aware of them.

● Walk slowly with awareness. Notice the sensation of lifting each leg forward, and placing your foot on the ground. Use this intentional type of walking as your anchor of attention. Occasionally pause after several steps to breathe and check in with your mind and body. What does the movement feel like? What does the ground feel like? Are you aware of any thoughts? Do you notice any impatience or resistance coming up?

● Briefly scan your body from your feet, to your legs, through the abdomen, around to the back, arms, chest, neck, face, and up to the crown of the head. Check in to notice any sensations you experience and what they feel like without trying to change anything. You can do this standing, sitting or lying down.

● Observe any thoughts or emotions, staying present to them. Shifting thoughts and emotions are like weather patterns in the body and mind and can affect how we feel.

● Without changing anything, be aware if your mind is making any judgments, analysis or comparisons—our minds do this naturally. Notice this habit and then gently bring your awareness back to the breath. Allow thoughts to come and go like clouds passing in the sky. Our thoughts can fuel emotions. Notice where you feel them in your body. These too will pass as we return to our anchor of attention.

● Look around slowly to notice any shapes, forms, patterns, textures, and light and dark values around you. Wherever you are, look up or down, and hold your gaze. See what you discover from this perspective. The more you look, the more you will see.

● Find an object that attracts you and observe it closely for a few minutes, including inspecting with a magnifying glass. Describe its qualities (just what you see, feel or hear) rather than categorizing or labeling it. This can bring you closer to its form and essence. You will develop more familiarity with it, perhaps even a friendliness.

As an experiment, try this with something you have difficulty with, such as an insect or even a person! Notice if you feel any initial urges to turn away or flee, and gently try to resist this. Describe its qualities without judging. After spending a little time with this, see if any of your discomfort has shifted.

● With your eyes, trace the shape of one or more objects you encounter. Tree branches make a good subject but you can do this with anything. It is a calming way to focus and center yourself with a visual anchor.

● Find something with an interesting texture and brush your fingers over it. Try closing your eyes while you do this and see if your awareness changes. What adjectives would you use to describe it? Later, you might use artwork to reconnect with what you have seen and felt.

- Send a message of loving-kindness, well-wishes, or appreciation to a plant, animal, or a person (even the earth if that feels comfortable). Notice how that feels in your mind and body. Draw, create other artwork, or write about how this experience was for you.

- Imagine that you are inside of and a part of a favorite plant, tree, animal, or even a person. Then imagine that it is inside of you. What does that connection feel like? Draw or write about this.

- Incorporate some of the same mindful awareness practices you've experienced here and apply them to some of your daily activities. Be aware of the continually shifting stimuli of the world around you, your senses, and how you feel in your body. You might wish to journal about what you experience.

We want to hear about your moments and images of wonder!
Describe your experience, where it was, what you were doing,
and how you felt. Send your stories to the email address below.

cathy@cathysacco.com

Time for Wonder

Cathy Sacco

you'll see the signs, birds on the branch and bees in the hive.
Be ver - y still, and hear ev - ery tree. Feel the wind
blow, it will help you be free.
Bb   C/F   F   F/A   Bb
Dm   C   Dm
C   F   Bb
F   Bb
f

Watch - ing a flow - er un - fold - ing with grace See so much more when you
slow down the pace.___ Wat - er the gar - den and each dif - f'rent seed.
Ev - ery - one blooms when they have what they need. No - tice the sun - light
shi - ning so bright, feet on the earth,___ and your mind like the sky.

Step back and pause,____ fo - cus in - side. Take a deep
breath and your heart o - pens wide.____________ You might think____ it will
last, but we on - ly____ have this mo - ment to treas - ure.____
Dm
C
Dm
B♭
C
B♭
F
B♭
F
F/C C
F
B♭

Take time for won-der, slow your-self down, plant-ing the seeds of love all a-round.

Written and Recorded by the Author
www.cathysacco.com/music/

ABOUT THE AUTHOR

Cathy Sacco is an experienced educator, mindfulness teacher and artist working at the intersection of human development, heath, spirituality and creativity. She consults with organizations to offer custom and evidence-based mindfulness programs, interventions and retreats for adults and youth to reduce stress, develop resilience, increase social-emotional intelligence and wellbeing. She has worked with cancer patients, survivors and caregivers, counselors, university faculty and students, medical students, K–12 teachers and youth, foster parents, business executives and the general public.

Cathy is on faculty at Xavier University's School of Childhood Education and holds an M.Ed from Xavier and AMS Montessori I-II credentials with experience as a Montessori classroom teacher. She is a qualified teacher of Jon Kabat-Zinn's evidence-based 8-week Mindfulness-Based Stress Reduction (MBSR) program through the Mindfulness Center at Brown University. Cathy is a certified Mindful Schools teacher and has also trained in Koru Mindfulness for emerging adults, .b Mindfulness In Schools Program, Mindful Self-Compassion through UCSD, and in contemplative practices through Naropa University's Authentic Leadership Program.

A local and national presenter on the topics of mindfulness and stress, self-compassion, arts integration and creativity, Cathy has been part of several research studies. She has had a personal meditation practice for many years, and is a member of the Being Peace Sangha.

Born on the banks of the Hudson in northern New Jersey, she currently lives in Cincinnati with her husband and two flown children. She has a creative arts studio at Brazee Street Studios.

PHOTO CREDITS

Pages   6, 9, 12, 15, 30, 32, 35, 42, 45, 50, 64, 67,
            69 top, 73, 88-89, 95, 101, 102, 103: by Cathy Sacco

Page 17: JSH

Page 24: "Slow" by Mason Bryant

Page 26: Jeff Oberst

Page 38: Tom Bradley

Page 99: Significant but unsuccessful attempts have been made to credit
          this photo appropriately

Page 110: Sherri Barber Photography

Remaining photos purchased through iStock, Shutterstock, Pexels, or Pixabay

www.cathysacco.com

*"Look deep into nature, and then you will
understand everything better."*

—Albert Einstein

*"The real voyage of discovery consists, not in seeking new
landscapes, but in having new eyes."*

—Marcel Proust